The Master Of The Feast...

Wilson R. Stearly

Nabu Public Domain Reprints:

You are holding a reproduction of an original work published before 1923 that is in the public domain in the United States of America, and possibly other countries. You may freely copy and distribute this work as no entity (individual or corporate) has a copyright on the body of the work. This book may contain prior copyright references, and library stamps (as most of these works were scanned from library copies). These have been scanned and retained as part of the historical artifact.

This book may have occasional imperfections such as missing or blurred pages, poor pictures, errant marks, etc. that were either part of the original artifact, or were introduced by the scanning process. We believe this work is culturally important, and despite the imperfections, have elected to bring it back into print as part of our continuing commitment to the preservation of printed works worldwide. We appreciate your understanding of the imperfections in the preservation process, and hope you enjoy this valuable book.

The Master of the Feast

By
WILSON R. STEARLY
Rector of the Church of the
Holy Apostles, Philadelphia

PHILADELPHIA
GEORGE W. JACOBS & CO.
PUBLISHERS

Copyright, 1912, by
GEORGE W. JACOBS & CO.
Published July, 1912

All rights reserved
Printed in U. S. A.

Prefatory Note

THIS little book, as whoever reads it will easily perceive, contains little that is original. Its incidents and stories are gathered together to point out the beauty of character of Him who was full of grace and truth. It is thought there may be a place for such a book, not a novel nor a manual of devotions. Why should not our young people find pleasure in reading what is not too sober or erudite, yet gives direction to eager thoughts and increase to earnest purposes? It was with those in mind who are yet fresh in the highway of life that these talks were first given. They are now sent forth in this form in the hope that those who read them may find therein strength and refreshment from the Master of the Feast.

Contents

I. His Feeling of Responsibility   7
II. His Resourcefulness   . .   37
III. His Opportunism . . . 63
IV. His Long View of Life . . 87
V. His Reward 113

I
HIS FEELING OF RESPONSIBILITY

I

HIS FEELING OF RESPONSIBILITY

THIS little book has to do with one of the miracles of Jesus. It is not intended to discuss the general question as to whether miracles can happen or not, nor what is the value of the miraculous element in the Gospels. There has been a distinct change in the attitude of the Christian world toward miracles in the last fifty years. In former days great apologetic use was made of the miracles. They were commonly cited as evidences of the deity of our Lord. In our day there are people in all the Christian churches who would be glad to eliminate entirely the miraculous element in the New Testament. They find it difficult to believe in the miracles. Some go so far as to say that they do not believe the miracles actually happened.

It is probable that most people in the Christian Church to-day do not occupy either of these positions. Taking Jesus to be the kind of a man described in the Gospels, it is natural, a great many think, to suppose that His life and ministry would be accompanied by great and wonderful works. There can be no doubt that those who reported the marvelous deeds of Jesus, which are called miracles, actually believed that they occurred. They were sensible and honest people, and any fair literary criticism has great difficulty in discounting or discrediting their reports. So that the majority of Christian people, while they by no means attach great significance to the miracles as proof of the deity of Jesus, yet, on the whole, are quite content to believe that they happened, and are glad that they are in the gospel story as records of the wondrous outpouring of the divine energy and love which resided in the personality of Jesus Christ.

It is probable, however, that the interest of most modern Christians in the miracles is not argumentative or speculative but practical. We are apt to ask, What do the miracles mean to us? When we study them, we wish to learn what effect they had on those for whose benefit they were wrought. That a blind man had his vision restored, a deaf man was enabled to hear and a lame man to walk —these were amazing and valuable accomplishments. But we would like to know something more; we are interested in the results. The question we ask is, How were the characters and after lives of these people affected by the good deeds done for them? That we have been through pain or pleasure, have had a long period of prosperity or adversity, does not matter so much as what remains in our life after these experiences. What life does with us, or to put it the other way, what we do with life, is more important than what life brings us. The intent of life is more significant than its content.

It is interesting to ask in regard to each of the miracles, What was its final outcome? What became afterward of the lepers who were cleansed? What did the deaf and the blind and the lame do with their restored powers?

More interesting than this is the consideration of what attributes of

His Feeling of Responsibility

character the miracles bear witness to in the personality of the one who worked them. I have in mind not those more outstanding qualities which we are tempted at once to think of, such as the powers displayed in them; for these belong to the mechanics of the miracles, and they are paralleled by a thousand mysterious and strange operations which are going on around us all the time. Water is being changed into wine every season, and the powers of resurgent life are continually in thousands of sick rooms and hospitals driving out the powers of death and disease. These are processes which contain insoluble mysteries. Like all the great and definite processes of creation and transformation they are beyond our perfect understanding. But we can with profit turn from this aspect of the miracles and consider them from another point of view. We can ask, What spiritual qualities do the miracles bear witness to in Jesus? What dispositions of the heart of the Master do they illustrate?

It is with this question in mind that we are in this little book to study one of Jesus' wonderful deeds. The miracle which I have chosen is the one which was thought of by the early Christians as typical and symbolic of all. It is the only one of the miracles of our Lord recorded by all four Evangelists. Each included it in his Gospel, not because it was the most stupendous miracle, but because it was the greatest sign. When they looked back over the ministry of Jesus, they recalled the occasion when it took place and all the surroundings of it as being a most characteristic scene in Jesus' life; and as prophetic and emblematic of

His Feeling of Responsibility

His continuing and abiding relation to His friends. It was a visible setting forth of Christ as the head of the Brotherhood. He was the Father of the family, the Master of the Feast, breaking the bread of life, and handing the celestial food to those who were dependent upon it for the very existence of their spiritual being. You will perceive that we are to study the miracle of the Loaves and Fishes; that the event we are to dwell upon is that in which one afternoon on the hillside by the Sea of Galilee Jesus fed a great multitude of people with five loaves and two fishes.

St. John in his remembrance of the occasion begins his description as follows: " Jesus, therefore lifting up His eyes, and seeing that a great multitude cometh unto Him, saith unto Philip, Whence are we to buy bread that these may eat?" St. Mark describes it in a little different fashion. He tells us that Jesus had gone with His disciples into the country for a little period of relief and rest, but they could not hide themselves from the multitude who had followed them in great eagerness; and when Jesus saw them gathered about Him, He felt compassion for them, as sheep not having any shepherd, and tired as He was, He went on teaching them during the long afternoon. Then when the day was drawing to its close, the sun was sinking toward the west, and the shadows of evening gathering around, the disciples came to Jesus and urged Him to send the multitude away. "There are great numbers of them," they argued, "and the day is far spent, and this is a desert place. You have taught them for many hours and they have no right

His Feeling of Responsibility

to expect anything more. Let them go now and care for themselves."

There you see in clear contrast the distinction between the human and the divine point of view; the worldly and the Christian attitude toward life. The disciples exhibit the worldly point of view at its best. We know what the worldly point of view is at its worst. There are men and women here and there about us who exemplify that view. They think the world is nothing more than a happy hunting-ground. They look upon all people and things as so many subjects for exploitation in their own interest. All we can say in regard to them is contained in Jesus' words, "Verily, they have their reward." But the disciples exhibit the worldly point of view at its best. There is a good bit of justification for the course they urged upon Jesus. He had done

His stint of work that day, more than His share in fact; why should He trouble further? "The place is desert and the day is now far spent; send them away, that they may go into the country and villages round about, and buy themselves somewhat to eat." Here is a plausible view of the situation, and sound advice from a good moral standpoint.

In this opinion and recommendation the disciples represent high moral excellence.

I have never been able to sympathize with the fashion which has obtained in some religious quarters of decrying certain types of character as being merely moral. We have no right to cast a slur upon morality of any sort. Indeed we have sore need in our day for the development of a sterner and more rigorous and amplified morality. There can be no human society, no useful and pleasant association of men with their fellows unless there are earnest endeavors upon the part of all to cultivate the primary and fundamental moral qualities. The four cardinal virtues are always worth striving for. Justice and Temperance and Prudence and Courage are worthful elements of character and must be part of the equipment of every one who wishes to live his life well.

But we ought not to be blind to the fact that Christianity implies something more than the possession of the four cardinal virtues; and this incident in the story of the miracle is instructive just because it presents so clear and well defined a contrast between the high-toned worldly-minded view of life and the Christian view of life.

There are two great words which

ought to signify and stand for much to every one. One word is Duty and the other is Love. I suppose Duty is the great word to the moralist. I am sure that Love is the great word to the Christian. Love is larger than duty; it commands a wider horizon, and entails a heavier responsibility. The Christian must share in the experience of Christ, who could not escape from the thought that He should provide, if He could, for the multitude of people around Him. He had a feeling of responsibility toward them; and every Christian must in greater or less degree share that feeling.

It is perfectly natural for us to protest against this. We find ourselves often saying, "Christianity demands too much of us." We are all in our hearts individualists. We believe that each one of us must give account of himself to God; we are apt to say that is the first and primary consideration; and we push other things to one side. We sympathize to some degree with those characters in the Bible who have by word or action expressed this view. Cain in the beginning of the Bible story cries out, " Am I my brother's keeper?" The prodigal in Jesus' parable starts upon his career saying, "Give me the portion of goods that falleth to me." The Priest and the Levite in the story of the Good Samaritan pass by the wounded man on the other side of the road. Voltaire puts it in attractive fashion for the modern man in his story of Candide, the moral of which is that the highest end of human striving is for each man to attend to his own garden.

But the world's saviours have been

those who have gone beyond duty, even in its highest and most widely moral sense.

Proof that a self-centered morality is not adequate for man is seen in the thrill which goes through our hearts whenever we hear of an unselfish act of service. I read not long ago an incident in the life of Dr. Grenfell, the Apostle of Labrador. Here is its description in his own words:

"Nearly three years ago I was going down south one day to answer a call in the winter in regard to a young boy of about sixteen who had a diseased hip and thigh. A message came in about the middle of Sunday. It was a very urgent case. We started at once with the dogs, and as it was very urgent and the going was very good, the ice being hard frozen, I took a very light sledge and just a few other things—

His Feeling of Responsibility

an axe and a rifle and some instruments—and started off alone. I shall never forget it. It was Easter Sunday, and the weather turned very bad before evening. I had to forego crossing an arm of the sea. I met a number of fishermen in a little hamlet by the side of the arm of the sea, and being Easter Sunday, we read about the life after death, and about how Christ's body was recognized and how His disciples expected to recognize one another, and about the realness that we had in our faith when life in Labrador or Hampstead is done. The next morning at daylight I crossed the ice, but as it so happened, the sea that had been in overnight had broken up the ice and the surface had frozen over, and without knowing it I was going over ice that would not carry. I struck the ice with my whip, and found it would not bear, but there was no turning round. We had to gallop as hard as we could, but it was no use; we all went through, the dogs and myself. There was nothing to do but to cut the dogs adrift and see if they could get ashore. By God's providence one of them climbed out on to a piece of ice, and I had his long trace tied to me round one of my wrists. We got out on the ice, and we drifted out to sea. All that night and part of next day I drifted off out of sight of land. There was only a small piece of ice left, and I knew that if any minute the ice broke my last minute had come. But it was not so. By God's providence the men had seen me overnight. I thought then of the reality of something that was so real, and on looking back on life, the joy of having had the honor of being allowed to

His Feeling of Responsibility

serve was so real, and the presence of God was so absolutely real and practical, that it bore me up. In the morning I hoisted a flag. I had to kill some of the dogs because I was soaked through and had hardly any clothes. I made a flagpole and put up my shirt as a flag, and some of these men who had seen me overnight managed to haul out a life-boat over the ice, and eventually came out and picked me up. These men were fishermen—great, big, strong men. They have seen lots of sorrows and troubles; they are not particularly given to sentiment; but every man, as he jumped on that small piece of ice as the boat came up alongside, took my hand and shook it, and cried and never said a word. It was joy that made them cry because they felt the reality of the joy they had in saving a man's life."

The Master of the Feast

You can easily see the point of this. These hardy fishermen did not have to do what they did, and Dr. Grenfell did not have to do what he was doing. Nobody would have found fault with either of them if they had stayed at home and lived lives of perfect security, of ease and comfort. But every man goes up in the scale of humanity and steps out from his humanity toward the divine life and character in proportion as he accepts responsibility, and acknowledges himself bound by some inward impulse to do and to dare, to suffer and to endure for the benefit and blessing of those who have no other claim upon him save that they are God's children and his brethren.

The question this incident in the miracle presents is this: Can you take your stand by Jesus' side in this particular? Is it possible for you in your relations with others, and in your attitude to the world in general, to cherish and to have the mind of Christ? Can you feel responsible for the wellbeing and the blessing of your world?

The way in which we are to realize this is by the extension of the moral and natural feelings which belong to us as men, beyond the narrow circle of the immediate relationships of life. It was finely said of Sir Walter Scott, "He speaks to every man as if they were blood-relations." That is what we have to try to do in our daily living.

One time Horace Mann, the great educator, delivered an address at the opening of a reformatory institution for boys. During the course of it, he remarked, "If only one boy is saved from ruin, it would pay for all the cost and care and labor of establishing such an institution." After

The Master of the Feast

the exercises were over, a gentleman approached Mr. Mann, and said to him, "Did you not color that a little when you said that all the expense and labor would be repaid if it only saved one boy?" "Not if it was my boy," was the solemn and convincing reply.

You see how that answer touches the heart of the Christian attitude toward life; how it explains why it was that Jesus should look out upon the multitude of people who were round about Him, and feel His heart grow tender toward them, and His purpose grow strong to minister to them to the utmost. That God was His Father was perfectly clear to Him, and that God was Father to all these men was also clear, and therefore they were His brethren, and He could do no less than all that was possible in their behalf.

His Feeling of Responsibility

It is perfectly clear that if we wish to be Christ's disciples, we must admit this principle into our hearts. We have got to realize that as the glory of Christ lay in the fact that though He was rich, yet for our sakes He became poor, and did all things of that divine love which was in the heart of God, which He expressed in all His earthly life and ministry,—so also if we would follow Him, we must cultivate the same feeling of responsibility for the wellbeing of others, which moved Him that bright afternoon when He would not send the people away hungry, but said to His disciples, "They have no need to go away; give ye them to eat."

There are two things which make it difficult for us always to carry this feeling of responsibility with us. In the first place the lives of most of us are so sheltered and protected that the actual sorrow and pain and need of the world does not get very close to us. We live perhaps in the best neighborhoods in the city. There are comparatively no homeless and vicious people breaking into our lives. When we go through the poorer sections of the city we sometimes see sights which cause us to think; but other scenes come quickly upon us, and those which are unpleasant are soon obliterated; and while we have something of sympathy for the afflicted and the poor, the keen realization of their sad estate is blunted and dimmed by the very richness and blessing of our lives. There is a striking passage in a speech made by David Lloyd-George, the Welsh Chancellor of the Exchequer, the foremost political orator of the English Liberal Party. In speaking of the men who composed the English House of Peers, he used these words: "They, in the main, are men to whom the eating of bread in the sweat of their brow is unknown. They are born within the magic circle of Cherubim with flaming swords, that guard the Paradise where plenty is obtained without labor. The care and the thought spent, the knowledge and the experience gathered, the skill acquired in the million ways of earning a living—that is no possession of theirs. The manna is strewn plenteously in their path through life, and others gather it for them. They do not sow; they do not reap; they do not mill the golden grain. About them I only say this—the brilliance of the sunshine of their lives blinds them to the squalor around them." The significance is in the last sentence. Very frequently does it happen that Christian people live so much in the sunshine of the good things of this world that they do not have in their hearts any notion of others' needs; are not conscious at all of the vice and sin, of the ignorance and sorrow that is in the world. But as friends of Christ, as His disciples, as those who wish to take our stand beside Him, we are bound to remember and to carry through our days as a great load the consciousness of the boys and girls and the men and women who are far away from the Father's house, and who need the ministering help of some elder brother, some tender shepherd, some brave-hearted saviour going forth to seek and to search for those who are lost.

Another obstacle in the way of our keeping alive day by day the sense of responsibility, which ought to characterize us as Christians, is the

The Feeling of Responsibility

monotony of the routine of our lives. Our relations with our fellows tend to become commonplace and ordinary. The struggle for existence obscures the romantic side of life; helps to make us oblivious to the high ministry for which we are responsible as the soldiers and servants of Christ. We live alongside of people all the time whose hearts are hungry, whose lives are not well filled with joy, and it is ours to minister to them, to supply them in some fashion with that heavenly manna upon which they might feed and so find strength and blessing, but we simply forget.

We must not ignore the needs of others, nor forget them. Our sense of responsibility for those about us must not be allowed to grow dull. We may never feel that we have done enough. We must have the spirit of the old Bishop who when

The Master of the Feast

asked by the Prince, from whose bounty he sought a favor for another, when his own turn would come, replied, "My turn is always come when I can serve another."

So it was with Jesus. When He came to Nazareth, where He had been brought up, to begin His public ministry, He went into the synagogue and applied to Himself the prophet's words: "The Spirit of the Lord is upon me, because he appointed me to preach good tidings to the poor: He hath sent me to proclaim release to the captives, and recovering of sight to the blind, to set at liberty them that are bruised. To proclaim the acceptable year of the Lord" (St. Luke 4: 18, 19). He took the needs of men upon Himself; their sorrows rested upon His heart. He felt He ought to help them; He accepted responsibility for them. When He saw

His Feeling of Responsibility

the multitude, He had compassion on them because they were as sheep not having a shepherd. And He said to Philip: "Whence are we to buy bread that these may eat?"

II
HIS RESOURCEFULNESS

II

HIS RESOURCEFULNESS

A YEAR or two ago there was published in the New York *Sun* an interview with the Hon. Charles Denby, who perhaps as well as any living American knows China and understands the Chinese character. In an interesting part of this interview, Mr. Denby recounted a conversation between Chang Chih-Tung, the Viceroy of Hupeh and Hunan, and William Barclay Parsons, the engineer of the New York Subway, who had gone to Hankow to make a preliminary survey for the Hankow-Canton Railway line. This was Mr. Parsons' first official call on the Viceroy before setting out on the survey, and Colonel Denby's description of the meeting is as follows:

"After the usual formal and platitudinous talk of a Chinese official interview, interspersed with plain suggestions that there were reasons for delay, the Viceroy apparently having some end to be gained by procrastination, the real business of the meeting was broached in these words of the Viceroy:

'Mr. Parsons, how many men are you taking on your survey?'

'Eight foreigners and four Chinese, your Excellency, not including the servants and escort.'

'It is not a large party, Mr. Parsons. There may be some difficulty with so few men.'

'It is large enough for my purpose, your Excellency.'

'You will remain here some

weeks making your arrangements, I suppose, Mr. Parsons. When, in fact, do you purpose to start?'

'To-morrow afternoon at one o'clock.'

At this there was a visible perturbation in the vice-regal mind, and a strong disposition to defeat this unheard-of promptitude in a Chinese undertaking became manifest. The Viceroy, in a tone which was meant to settle the matter, said, 'You can't leave here to-morrow. You will require at least ten days to get together your provisions and outfit.'

'The outfit is already arranged for,' answered the American engineer. 'A boat fully provisioned, capable of accommodating the whole party and containing everything necessary for the expedition, has been dispatched to-day to wait for us 120 miles up the river. My party will leave to-morrow and join her in about five days where the survey line touches the river.'

'Well, even so, I don't want you to leave so soon. I have much more to say to you and shall insist on several interviews.'

'Very well. I will remain here and report to you as often as you wish, and after several days I will follow the party by steam launch.'

The Viceroy showed visible annoyance at the failure of his last suggestion, and changed his grounds to an intimation of danger for the party. He said: 'The route your party proposes to travel over is not along the highways, and you will find many people unfamiliar with foreigners who may mistrust their motives and make trouble. You must keep your surveyors here until I can send out and explain the friendly purpose of the expedition.'

'It is not necessary,' said Mr. Parsons, ' to do any work of this kind among the people in the territory between this city and the place where we will reach our boat. I have had an exploring party of three foreigners over the line for the past week, and they returned last night, reporting the most friendly reception everywhere. The survey party will leave at one o'clock to-morrow, and I will join it by steam launch four days later. In the meantime, I am at your Excellency's orders.'

The Viceroy had no further pretext to offer, and the expedition started at one o'clock the next day."

Here is illustrated what we take pleasure in believing is a characteristic American trait. We like to

The Master of the Feast

think that the American, wherever he finds himself, and under whatever conditions, is able to take care of himself, has a good idea of what he wants to do, and can see it through to its completion.

This is a trait that is an essential element of the Christian character. It is illustrated in the story we are studying. We have seen how the Evangelist St. John described Jesus' sense of responsibility toward the multitude of people who were gathered around Him. Let us now look a bit further into our Lord's mind; let us note what thought and purpose was born of His consciousness of obligation to others. "Jesus, therefore lifting up His eyes, and seeing that a great multitude cometh unto Him, saith unto Philip, whence are we to buy bread that these may eat?" "And this He said to prove him, for He Himself knew what He would do."

There you see an attitude of mind very similar to that just illustrated in the case of the American engineer. Jesus, looking out upon the crowd, felt that He had resources in Himself; and in the same moment, the plan of His ministry to the multitude began to take shape in His mind. You may note this trait of character in all the stories and incidents of our Lord's life which are recorded in the Gospels. He is always prepared and ready. In the very beginning, as St. John tells us in the story of the Marriage Feast in Cana of Galilee, His mother exhibits confidence in His resourcefulness as she comes to Him saying, "They have no wine." In quite other circumstances, the same thing is portrayed in the interview recorded in the third chapter

The Master of the Feast

of St. John's Gospel. There you have Jesus talking to one of the most learned men of his time, a member of the national Sanhedrin, a Pharisee of the Pharisees, a scribe well instructed in the law, and Jesus is able to satisfy him too.

So wherever He goes, you find men instinctively turning toward Him; and as you read the Gospels you receive the impression that He never failed them. He had always within Himself some power and some resourcefulness which went forth to meet them in the place where they were and to satisfy their needs.

Now this is a quality which every one who wishes to live as a Christian must endeavor to possess. It is all very well to have a great feeling of responsibility toward those who are round about us, but it is quite possible for that feeling to dissipate itself in emotion. There are Christian people in the world who never accomplish very much definitely; not because they do not feel obligation and responsibility, but because they fail to formulate for themselves some definite plan for meeting their responsibility in concrete fashion.

The world is quite just in demanding that Christian people shall authenticate themselves as Christians by service to their fellows. The great Italian patriot, Mazzini, once said, "When I hear any one called good, I ask, Who then has he saved?" And the hard-headed people of the world rightly enough maintain the same point of view. Such men have not a great deal of sympathy with the enclosed nun who spends her days and years in prayer and meditation; and cannot swallow very well the man whose Christian service does not extend beyond taking part in experience meetings or reading the services of the church.

It may be true that the great development of Social Service as a part of young people's lives in our day is due in not a small degree to the feeling that, in connection with certain benevolent institutions, a person who wishes to serve his fellows may find a better opportunity than in connection with the Christian Church. Of course Social Service has become more or less of a fad, and there are a good many young men and women who take it up nowadays because they think it is the proper thing to do; but there are others who have gone into it with a sincere and earnest desire to do something useful for their fellow men; to put out at interest the talents with which God has endowed them. All such service is really Christian. It may not always be done explicitly in the name of Christ, but it is certainly in the spirit of Him who when He made His first appearance in Nazareth, after He had received Baptism at the hands of John, stood up and read from the Old Testament that splendid passage in Isaiah: "The Spirit of the Lord is upon Me. He has anointed Me to do useful service to men."

And we Christian men believe that none of us, who wish sincerely to follow Christ, may evade the obligation to turn our feeling of responsibility for others, which we get from Him, into the way of some definite service for our fellows. In the Creed we declare our expectation of being judged by Him who is our Master and our Lord, and whose life is fitly summed up in a phrase in the New

The Master of the Feast

Testament as being that of one "who went about doing good."

"'I made life sweet,' my Lord will say,
When we meet at the end of the King's highway.
'I smoothed the paths where thorns annoy,
I gave the mother back her boy;
I mended the children's broken toy.
And what did you?' my Lord will say
When we meet at the end of the King's highway.

"'I showed men God,' my Lord will say,
'As I traveled along the King's highway.
I eased the sister's troubled mind;
I helped the blighted to be resigned;
I showed the sky to the souls grown blind.
And what did you?' my Lord will say
When we meet at the end of the King's highway."

It is good to dwell upon this particular moment in the story of Christ's feeding of the multitude. As these people drew near to Him, they ap-

His Resourcefulness

pealed to His sense of responsibility. He felt that He owed them something. He wished to supply their need. And as we look into His heart and mind, we can see that instantly there arose a certain plan; there came an idea as to the way in which He could meet His responsibility and do something to supply their lack.

Now a question always facing us, and particularly a question for young men and women, is this: What do you propose to do with your life? What kind of resources have you, and how far have you made any plan for taking your stand by the side of Christ in the way of definite service to your world?

There are two gifts which we may offer to the world which are of supreme worth and value. The first of them is the gift of a good and noble character. This is the most

The Master of the Feast

important thing that we can contribute. More important than what we say or what we do is what we are. It is a great thing for a man to be bigger than his job. Stanley speaks of occasions when, as Dean of Westminster Abbey, he had often to preach funeral sermons when the occasion was greater than the man. We all of us are desirous of having bigger and better positions, but we would do better if we began to purpose to be bigger and better individuals. Then the positions would take care of themselves. I have an idea that in the hurly-burly and rush of life we sometimes forget that the most precious gift we can offer and the very best service we can render to our world, is in striving for the upbuilding and development of a well-rounded and splendid personality.

His Resourcefulness

There was published recently the religious correspondence of William Ewart Gladstone. In his journal for 1830, that is in his twenty-fifth year, there is this entry: "In practice the great end is that the love of God may become the habit of my soul, and particularly these things are to be sought: 1. The spirit of love. 2. Of self-possession. 3. Of purity. 4. Of energy." Now there is exhibited a right sturdy and splendid consciousness of what personality is for, and the aims which a noble-minded young man may cherish concerning his life. Compare with that the purely material striving which absorbs the time of many people; or the constant endeavoring to amuse and entertain themselves, which takes up all the spare and leisure hours of many others.

There are many of us who are not half earnest and serious enough about life; and particularly we do not appreciate as keenly as we might how splendid is the opportunity that life affords for the building up of a great and noble type of character. Dr. Sven Hedin, in recounting his travels in Tibet, speaks of going to a Holy Mountain around which hundreds of pilgrims from remote parts of Asia were wearily trudging. When asked why they were doing this the reply was that so they hoped to find salvation. Another traveler in Tibet speaks of observing near a monastery a hole in a wall near the ground. Placed under it was a platter with some coarse food on it. Presently a shriveled gaunt hand was seen to be thrust through the hole and the food taken. "Who lives down there?" asked the traveler. "A very holy man," was the reply. "How long has he been in that dungeon?" "Twenty-five years." "Has he ever been out?" "No." "Will he ever come out?" "Not until he is carried out a dead man."

Now I imagine we should all conclude that these are mistaken ways in which to seek for salvation; but there is something magnificent about the greatness of desire and the earnestness of purpose which characterizes them. It is perhaps true that in this respect the people of the East excel those of the West. It may be this will be the great element which the people of the Orient will contribute to the final perfecting of the Christian character.

It has been remarked of Kipling's soldier characters that they are alluring and entertaining personalities. They are men of hardihood and courage. They are unselfish to a degree and willing to obey orders to the last moment; but you miss in them a something which characterized the earlier generation of English civil and military servants. What you miss is a consciousness of purpose. They will do their work faithfully, but they do not see and cherish for themselves a great purpose of accomplishment; and it is in this that character lies.

Character is the consciousness of purpose, and the best character is the consciousness of a high and serious purpose. That is the first thing that as Christians we have to strive for. That is the primary gift which we ought to endeavor to offer to the world.

> "The dear Lord's best interpreters
> Are characters and souls;
> The gospel of a Christlike life
> Is more than books or scrolls."

The second thing that we must

His Resourcefulness

strive for if we wish to take our stand by Jesus' side is to bring our character to bear upon some definite problem; to put our time and strength in at some particular point; to accept as ours the obligation to relieve some individual burden, to meet some special need in the world. We have got to aim to make our service count. There are innumerable opportunities in the world for doing this. Sometimes there are calls which come to us to leave our home and our friends, and to serve in obscure and out-of-the-way places, and in unobserved fashion. I read the other day the story of the man who gave a language to the Chippewas. His name was James Evans, and in the '40's of the last century he was a Methodist missionary stationed on Lake Winnipeg away up in Canada. He took the Cree language, invented characters for it, reduced it to simplicity, and to-day every member of that great tribe can learn to read and write his own language in a day. When Lord Dufferin, the Governor-General of Canada, was making a tour of the Northwest a few years ago, and was told of this man's work, he said enthusiastically: "There have been buried in Westminster Abbey with national honors many men whose claims to fame have been far less than those of this devoted missionary—the man who taught a whole nation to read and write." So God calls men now and again into hard and difficult service in remote and unknown places; and we must strive by all that is high and holy, when such a call comes to us, to answer it nobly and say, "Here am I, Lord. Send me."

His Resourcefulness

But for the most part life is so ordered that men find their opportunities for service in the place where they are; and heaven knows there are enough chances to do definite and noble bits of service round about every one of us. The churches to which we belong need workers. The neighborhoods in which we live may be served. The city in which our lot is cast demands the thoughts and prayers and manful endeavors toward righteousness of many men and women. There is enough to be done. The question is will we have first the consciousness of our responsibility; and then will we have eyes to see, and minds to conceive, and hearts to will, and purpose to do and dare for the Kingdom of Heaven's sake? It is not possible to point out any particular thing which any one of us is bound to do; manifestly that is a matter which every individual must determine for himself. But we shall have done well if out of our study of the mind of Christ there arises within us an urgent and insistent impulse toward the service of those about us. To have resources in constant readiness; and to be developing all the time, as we go on, fine and well-considered plans of action, definite and concrete forms of service; this is our obligation and our duty as the soldiers and servants of Christ. There is a little poem of Edward Everett Hale's called "The Unnamed Saints," which tells the story of many who have served well in their day and generation. To emulate their spirit and follow their example is to be included among the elect of God.

His Resourcefulness

"What was his name? I do not know his name.
  I only know he heard God's voice and came;
    Brought all he loved across the sea,
    To live and work for God and me;
      Felled the ungracious oak,
      With horrid toil
      Dragged from the soil
  The thrice-gnarled roots and stubborn rock;
  With plenty filled the haggard mountainside,
  And, when his work was done, without memorial died.
  No blaring trumpet sounded out his fame;
  He lived, he died. I do not know his name.

"No form of bronze and no memorial stones
  Show me the place where lie his mouldering bones.
    Only a happy city stands,
    Builded by his hardened hands;—
      Only ten thousand homes,
      Where, every day,
      The cheerful play
  Of love and hope and courage comes;
  These are his monuments, and these alone,
  There is no form of bronze and no memorial stone.

The Master of the Feast

"And I? Is there some desert or some
    boundless sea
  Where Thou, Great God of angels, wilt send
    me?
    Some oak for me to rend, some sod
      For me to break,
  Some handful of Thy corn to take,
    And scatter far afield,
      Till it in turn shall yield
        Its hundredfold
      Of grains of gold,
  To feed the happy children of my God?
Show me the desert, Father, or the sea;
If that Thine Enterprise? Great God, send
    me!
And though this body lie where ocean rolls,
Father, count me among All Faithful Souls."

III
HIS OPPORTUNISM

III

HIS OPPORTUNISM

ONE of the most trying kinds of people to work with are the sort who are always discontented with the circumstances of their jobs. There are some persons who are always finding fault with the materials they have to work with. They are always laying the blame for imperfect work upon the conditions under which it had to be done. But the proof of a great artist is that he is able to get fine results from comparatively poor materials. The artist spirit consists not only in setting perfection as one's aim, but in striving to attain perfection under untoward circumstances.

The Bible is one of the most romantic books in literature. The romance that runs all through it is the story of "the so-much from the so-little." What is illustrated in the traditions of the great heroes of the Bible is the wondrous possibility that lies before those who with faith and courage manfully take up the problems of their life. The glory of the divine in man is the glory of the great accomplishment from the small and insignificant beginnings. You see this illustrated in the story of Abraham, the wandering pilgrim who became the father of a great multitude of faithful souls. You see it in the story of Joseph, the Jewish slave-boy who became prime minister; and in the story of David, the shepherd lad who succeeded at last in establishing himself on the throne of a kingdom.

This is the romantic side of the

story of Jesus. The carpenter becomes the Saviour of the world. A fairly good title for the Gospels, if they were to be published first in our modern day, would be " From the manger by the hill of Calvary to the throne of God."

This is the thought to which we must next direct our attention in connection with the story of the feeding of the multitude. When our Lord had accepted in His mind responsibility for those who had gathered around Him, and when He had decided that He would make a great venture of faith, He looked around for the materials to work with. His disciples had found a small boy with five loaves and two fishes, and they had succeeded in getting him to put them at their disposal. But they said deprecatingly to Christ, " What are these among so many ? " And then we read these significant words, "Jesus therefore took the loaves." Here is indicated another quality in the mind of Jesus which we as His disciples must endeavor to emulate in our daily lives. We have got to learn to make the most of what we have. We must cultivate the spirit which is not disdainful of what God has given us, but which is able to take it and use it to the very best advantage.

There are two praiseworthy endeavors which at one time or another we almost all of us are called upon to make. One is to take ourselves out of certain circumstances and surroundings. A man came to me once asking if I could get him a position. I suggested that he already had a position in a shop where he had been employed for quite a while. He replied that he knew that this was

His Opportunism

so, but he said, "I must get away from it, and I am willing to take almost any kind of work in order to get out of that place." And when I asked the reason for this determination, he told me that it was a case, it seemed to him, of the saving of his soul. "It is worse than hell there. The things that I must hear and the things that I must see burn themselves into my mind and heart and drive out all the higher thoughts and impulses which I wish to cherish," was his reply. I imagine that happens a good many times in life. Young men and young women in the business world find that the moral atmosphere of the shop or office or store in which they have to pass so many hours of their day is such as to injure the finer sensibilities and impulses of their natures. Jesus said once, "If thy right hand causeth thee to stumble, cut it off, and cast it from thee: for it is profitable for thee that one of thy members should perish, and not thy whole body be cast into hell." There is a kind of heroic surgery which we must all apply now and again in life. We had better do with less and save our souls alive, than stay where we are and find ourselves steadily deteriorating. There are places of employment, and there are associations, from which now and again we have to flee for our very lives, as Lot and his family turned their backs upon Sodom and fled to the mountains.

Far more frequently it is our duty to stay where we are, and facing boldly the conditions under which we have to work, strive manfully to make the very utmost that is possible out of them for our own good and the good of others. Mostly when we walk up to the great Master and ask for a new job and better pay He inquires whether we have made as much as we could out of our present situation. It is perfectly natural for us to think that we could do better under other conditions. We all of us possess in greater or less degree the faculty of imagination, by the exercise of which we frame ideal pictures of the conditions in which other people live. There is hardly a clergyman, I suppose, who does not sometimes think of certain brother clergymen with envy, conceiving their situation and work to be so much preferable to his own. Many a young woman in a shop or store, as she deals with her customers, thinks to herself what an easy time they are having, and how joyous and pleasant life must be for them. But over against this tendency of our imagination is the fact that we are where we are, and that we are bound as Christians to try faithfully to do our duty in that state of life in which it has pleased God to set us. The fact that we are where we are creates a strong presumption in favor of our staying there and working out our life and destiny in that place.

A question which often arises in our minds, and which is difficult to answer, is whether on the whole most people get their just deserts in this world. Sometimes we think they do; and then again when we walk along certain streets in a great city, and when we think of certain persons the circumstances of whose lives we have known intimately, we think that in this world it is not true that every one gets all that he deserves. But the discussion of such a question leads far afield; and it is more useful

His Opportunism

to ask ourselves whether we can take our stand by Jesus' side in making the most of what has been given us; accepting the circumstances and conditions in which we find ourselves, not apathetically, or with a low-visioned contentment, but with a great purpose to transform our circumstances, to use them in such fashion that through them we may find a way into fellowship with God.

There are two things necessary in order to do this. The first of them is insight. Every job holds us in proportion as we see its potentialities. Any sort of work in which we could see no possible connection between the details of it and its working out for good in our own life or the lives of others, would become commonplace and monotonous and intolerable before long. But there are not many jobs of that sort. It is probably true that there is no situation so hard, no work so narrow and circumscribed, but that in connection with it there are some possibilities for useful service to others. Lord Shaftsbury to the day of his death carried a common silver watch which had been given to him by a woman who had been his nurse in his childhood days. He does not tell us her name even ; but he is a living witness to the abiding influence upon his life and character of what she said and did when with him in the most impressionable and formative period of his life. Who does not know the story of Brother Lawrence, the Monk of the Carmelite Monastery in Paris, who passed his days among pots and kettles and pans, but who so turned his kitchen into a chapel of the Holy Spirit that he has led multitudes into that blessed discipline called "the practice of the presence of God"?

It is possible for us to disdain our life and its details when we look upon it superficially, to say concerning it and its opportunities what the disciples said about the five loaves and two fishes; but it is also possible, if we have insight, to perceive the spiritual and eternal elements in the material and temporary aspects of the day's work. We begin life with great ideals; and quite a period in every right-thinking young person's life is devoted to heroic efforts to realize the ideal. I would not give much for any young person who is not a great idealist. It looks bad for a young man or young woman to be blasé and disillusioned. But as the years go by, experience teaches us that the realization of the ideal is a most difficult, perhaps an impossible thing; so we turn the tables and say to ourselves, What we must strive to do is to idealize the real. As Browning puts it:

"The common problem—yours, mine, every one's,
Is—not to fancy what were fair in life
Provided it could be,—but, finding first
What may be, then find how to make it fair
Up to our means."

Our aim must be not to realize the ideal, but to idealize the real; which means not building all sorts of airy and beautiful castles in Spain, but looking steadily and clearly upon life in an endeavor to see what are its real forces and powers; what are the abiding and spiritual goods which are wrapped up in the temporary and fleeting experiences. St. Paul puts it in this way: "We look not at the things which are seen, but at the things which are not seen, for the things which are seen are temporal, but the things which are not seen are eternal." A modern rhymster, whose name I do not know, has brought this same thought into touch with every-day life in these lines:

> "It isn't raining rain to me,
>   It's raining daffodils;
> In every dimpled drop I see
>   Wild flowers on the hills,
> And clouds of gray engulf the day,
>   And overwhelm the town;
> It isn't raining rain to me,
>   It's raining roses down.
>
> "It isn't raining rain to me,
>   But fields of clover-bloom,
> Where any buccaneering bee
>   May find a bed and room.
> A health unto the happy,
>   A fig for him who frets.
> It isn't raining rain to me,
>   It's raining violets."

The second thing we must do if we wish to make the most of our opportunities is to live in the power of this spirit. We have to be making every day a great venture of faith. We have got to assume that life is worthful, and that in any and every situation, under every given set of circumstances, there are immense possibilities for us. In the neighborhood in which I live there are people who are so poor that during the winter they have to buy their fuel by the bucketful. I noticed one day a wagon of a good colored brother who peddles coal from street to street during the winter months. He walked along with a jaunty air and happy mien, which was reflected in the words which he had printed on the side of his wagon. There was his name in clear letters, and the announcement of his business as a coal dealer, and underneath the following legend: "God's ways is ways of pleasantness, and all His paths is peace." Now it may have been that this was an ostentatious advertising of his religion. It is possible that under cover of such a pious sentiment he might occasionally take advantage of his customers by giving short measure; but it struck me at the time as I looked at the man that the words were an evidence of the possession by him of a fine and victorious spirit. He was one of those who seemed to be master of their lives.

There is a great difference between being master of your life and being mastered by it; and the way to be master is to live your life in the power of some great idea or purpose. If you can carry into your work and toil day by day some splendid idea and some abiding purpose, you will find that gradually the details and the drudgery of the day's work will fall into their places and contribute to your peace and happiness.

This is illustrated in the point we are considering in this story. What made our Lord great in that moment, and what enabled Him perhaps to do the great things that He did for this multitude of men, was that He was completely possessed by a great idea. Supposing that, when He had gotten the loaves, He had calmly stuck them under His coat, and beckoning quietly to one and another of His friends, had gone away into some retired corner to satisfy their own pressing needs. Had He done this He could not have blessed the multitude that day. If that had been His spirit and His temper He could not have become the Saviour of the world. It was true of Him then, what was afterward said of Him in taunting fashion as He hung upon

His Opportunism

the cross: "He saved others; Himself He could not save." That was the great idea that possessed Him; and in the power of that idea He could take the most meager materials and transform them and multiply them until they satisfied the needs of a great multitude.

Can we do that? Can we take our stand alongside of our Master Christ in this? Can we be Christian opportunists, committing our lives right here and now to the principle of making the best of what we have? Goethe in his story makes his hero cry out, "America is here or nowhere." In the history of the Roman Empire, there was a day when the Senate was deliberating whether to remove the seat of government to the newly-conquered town of Veii, when the debate was interrupted by the rattle of arms in the vestibule, and

The Master of the Feast

the voice of an officer was heard saying, "Plant the standard here."

It is not always easy to do this with our lives. It is not right, or always wise to minimize the hardships and difficulties and burdens and sorrows which many of us have to face day by day. But it is perfectly sure and certain that the way out is not found by seeking to escape, but by pressing boldly to the front, and with the spirit of hardy courage, saying, "Here I will endeavor, here I will strive to conquer by God's good grace."

> "Forenoon and afternoon and night,—Forenoon
> And afternoon and night,—Forenoon, and—what!
> The empty song repeats itself. No more?
> Yea, that is life: make this forenoon sublime,
> This afternoon a psalm, this night a prayer,
> And Time is conquered, and thy crown is won."

His Opportunism

There is another consideration which must be added to what we have already suggested. We must never forget that if we strive earnestly and faithfully great things must result. The point of this incident in our story is the romance of "the so-much from the so-little." It is the miracle which we see repeated every year as seeds are dropped into the ground and spring up and bring forth thirty and sixty and an hundred fold. We see the same wonderful transformation and progress illustrated every now and then in the world of trade. I read the other day a sketch of the career of Lord Mount-Stephen. He began life as a herd-boy in Scotland. Then he was a draper's apprentice. Afterward he worked as an assistant clerk in a St. Paul's churchyard shop. Then he decided to try his luck in Canada, and found there, in the shape of the Canadian-Pacific Railway, the means of acquiring colossal wealth. And now every year just before Christmas the King and Queen of England, the sovereigns of the English Empire, are entertained by Lord Mount-Stephen and his wife in Brocket Hall. There are cases analogous to that which we hear of from time to time. Occasionally we feel that the opportunities for success and advancement are growing less; but there still remain many worlds to conquer, and a multitude of avenues open out to great achievement.

We must never forget that what is true in the material and earthly realm is no less true in regard to the higher parts of our nature. It is always possible for us starting where we are to make use of what we have; to do and to dare and to accomplish great things. There are no good causes that are lost; there are no hopeless lives. The one question is, Have we faith and will? Have we courage and abiding trust in God? Can we take the loaves of our life and under the power of a great and transfiguring idea, use them as the children of God?

"This I beheld, or dreamed it in a dream—
There spread a cloud of dust along a plain;
And underneath the cloud, or in it, raged
A furious battle, and men yelled, and swords
Shocked upon swords and shields. A prince's banner
Wavered, then staggered backward, hemmed by foes.
A Craven hung along the battle's edge,
And thought, 'Had I a sword of keener steel—
That blue blade that the King's son bears —but this
Blunt thing——!' he snapt and flung it from his hand,

The Master of the Feast

And lowering crept away and left the field.
Then came the King's son, wounded, sore bestead,
And weaponless, and saw the broken sword,
Hilt-buried in the dry and trodden sand,
And ran and snatched it; and with battle-shout
Lifted afresh he hewed the enemy down,
And saved a great cause that heroic day."

IV

HIS LONG VIEW OF LIFE

IV

HIS LONG VIEW OF LIFE

Two further elements of Jesus' character come incidentally into view as we follow the story. The first of them is His wisdom and sagacity. I should like to use the word cleverness, except that that word falls far below the dignity and splendor which associate themselves in our thoughts with the mind of Christ.

We read in the Gospel that when the loaves and fishes had been found, Jesus, accepting responsibility for the multitude and conscious of His purpose, knowing what He was going to do, said to His disciples, "Make the men sit down." There is significance in this phrase. It is easy for us to perceive it if we stop to think a moment. It is not irreverent for us to believe that Jesus was a great artist. He knew how important is the manner in which things are done. I suppose many of the endeavors of good people fail to bring forth good results because they are undertaken in the right spirit, but in the wrong way. A modern thinker, in a mood tinged with skepticism, has said that one of the standing miracles of Christianity is that the Christian religion has survived so much of its teaching.

As Jesus planned for His great service to the multitude, He instinctively realized how important it was that every man should be in a receptive state of mind; that what He proposed to do should be done in such a fashion that all should be able to see in a moment the significance and purport of it. So He has them all sit down in groups upon the grass, and rising before them, in full view of every man, He takes the loaves in His hand; and then with a characteristic movement of His body, which all of the evangelists have noted, He begins His wonderful work. In each of the Gospels it is said that "He looked up to heaven." There was significance in that. It was one of those actions which speak louder than words. The expression of His face, the movement of His eyes, spoke wonders to those who were around Him. They perceived as by a flash of insight that in His heart was gratitude to God the heavenly Father for what had been bestowed. And then as He began to break and to give away the fragments of the loaves, their hearts were stirred within them at the miracle of divine love.

The Master of the Feast

It has been thought by some students of the Bible that the greatest miracle that day on the shore of Galilee was that which was wrought in the hearts of the multitude, who learned a great lesson of self-forgetting love.

It is perhaps true, as the Scripture has it, that "the children of this world are in their generation wiser than the Children of Light," but it ought not to be so. There is no reason why, when we purpose to do a good work, we should not plan to do it in the wisest and best fashion possible. The Master urged His disciples to be as wise as serpents and as harmless as doves. It is only right and just, it is only part of a Christian's equipment, that he should bring to bear on the problems of his Christian life and service the best wisdom and sagacity with which

His Long View of Life

God has endowed him. It is possible that the Church and many good movements for human betterment fail to attain their greatest sweep of usefulness because men of capacity and ability do not bring their intellectual powers to the service of the great cause.

Another element of Jesus' character appears in the words which He spoke to His disciples when the miracle was over and the work was done. We read that after every one had been satisfied, He said to His disciples, "Gather up the broken pieces that remain over, that nothing be lost." What do these words say to us about the mind of Christ? I think they illustrate what may be called Jesus' long view of life.

Business people will understand at once what is meant by that phrase.

There are two methods of doing

business. One is to work a proposition for all it is worth for this week or this month or this year, without regard to any consequences other than the gaining of the utmost possible profit in a given time, with the expectation of throwing the whole business upon the scrap heap after that. On the other hand, the greater part of the business world to-day regards it not only as more honorable, but in the long run more profitable to do business not for a month or a year, but for a decade and a generation. In the beginning the profits may not be so great, but when you consider the returns of many years, the better method is to be thinking to-day about to-morrow; to be dealing with customers in such a fashion this year that they will wish to trade with you again when the next season comes around. There is no doubt, I imagine, that this is the higher toned view of business, the one which commends itself to the good judgment of the best men in the commercial and manufacturing world.

This was what was in Jesus' mind that day. It was as though He thought the disciples might be tempted to conceive that this same sort of thing might go on at other times. He knew that it would not be so; that after this great experience there would come ordinary and commonplace days in which there would be no marvelous discovery and multiplication of provision for themselves and the multitude. He realized that every one needs, to make his life a success as a whole, some power which will carry him through dark and gloomy days upon which there come no inspirations and no outpourings of unexpected strength.

The Master of the Feast

The test of life comes in such days. And it is well for us to anticipate their coming, to recognize the periodic aspect of life, and to be ready against the days of dearth.

> "We cannot kindle when we will
>   The fire that in the heart resides;
> The spirit bloweth and is still,
>   In mystery our soul abides;
> But tasks in hours of insight will'd
> Can be through hours of gloom fulfill'd."

If we can provide strength in advance for our times of need, we shall do well.

A great part of religion consists in living up to the best that we know day by day, but another equally important element is living in such fashion to-day that to-morrow we shall find ourselves coming upon new sources of strength. One time Jesus said to His disciples, "Be not anxious for to-morrow, for the morrow shall take care of the things of itself." And then again He said, "Lay up for yourselves treasures in heaven." At another time, "Make to yourselves friends by means of the mammon of unrighteousness; that, when it shall fail, they may receive you into the eternal tabernacles." This, then, is a fair interpretation of Jesus' mind as expressed in these words. He believed in the conservation of forces. There was a kind of splendid economy in His nature. He thought of life as cumulative, and all of one piece.

Now this is a good thing for us to remember concerning our Christian life. I once knew a man who years before had sold to a great educational institution the ground upon which the buildings were located, and every year thereafter, at the annual commencement exercises of the college, he occupied a prominent position upon the platform and posed as a benefactor of the institution. But one good deed does not suffice to make a man a philanthropist. Neither is one religious experience enough to make a Christian. You must go on having religious experiences. There must be development and growth and progress through all the days. Dr. Stanley Hall once remarked that children who have become consciously religious at an early period of their lives reminded him of those good people who take great pride in getting up early. In the morning they go about bragging to everybody concerning the early hour at which they have risen, but they are apt to be very tiresome and sleepy all the rest of the day.

Probably many of us have met people who have had to look back-for the best experiences of their religious life. Something great and wonderful happened to them at a certain time, but the thing did not go on and develop. But it is said that we ought not to be weary in well-doing; and the crown of life is promised to those who are faithful unto death. It is a fatal thing for any one to rest on his laurels, or to have to turn his face to the past for his best days. Jesus, it would seem, was always looking ahead. He was conscious that there would be another day, and He wished to put His disciples in the way of being prepared for it. The way to go ahead is to gather up to-day and carry over into the morrow all that you can.

Jesus, I suppose we might say, believed in the grace of continuance. There is an interesting verse at the end of the first chapter of the Book of Daniel. In that chapter you will remember, perhaps, the description of the heroic stand taken by Daniel and his boy friends who in the palace of their captivity purposed not to defile themselves with the king's meat. After the narration of that story, we read at the very close of the chapter these words: "And Daniel continued even unto the reign of King Cyrus." Now that is a great tribute to Daniel, and expresses something fine about his character. He kept on through one reign after another, through many different experiences, and through years of ups and downs, the same sturdy and noble character when as an old man he opened his windows and prayed toward Jerusalem as he was when he was a boy. I believe we should all like to emulate Daniel in this respect.

There is a phrase in the service for

the administration of Holy Baptism which always makes a great impression upon my mind. When the child has been baptized, and while the priest still holds him in his arms, he marks upon his forehead the mystical sign of the cross, and with it, he utters these meaningful words, " We receive this child into the congregation of Christ's flock; and do sign him with the sign of the Cross, in token that hereafter he shall not be ashamed to confess the faith of Christ crucified, and manfully to fight under His banner, against sin, the world, and the Devil; and to continue Christ's faithful soldier and servant unto his life's end." Do you not think that these are great words at the ending? It was perhaps with them in mind that Keble wrote those fine lines which are in his poem for one of the Sundays in Advent:

The Master of the Feast

"Think not of rest; tho' dreams be sweet
Start up, and ply your heavenward feet.
Is not God's oath upon your head,
Ne'er to sink back on slothful bed,
Never again your loins untie,
Nor let your torches waste and die.
Till, when the shadows thickest fall,
Ye hear your Master's midnight call?"

There are two enemies to the grace of continuance in the Christian life. The first of them is the decline of enthusiasm. Almost every one has read Wordsworth's great poem on "Immortality," which begins with the suggestion that birth is an awakening and life a forgetting. We come trailing clouds of glory; but as the years go on, the consciousness of a wondrous past slips away from memory.

"The youth who daily farther from the east
 Must travel still is nature's priest.
  And by the vision splendid
  Is on his way attended;
At length the man perceives it die away,
And fade into the light of common day."

His Long View of Life

What the poet thus suggests as true of life in general takes place often enough in religious experiences. There are numbers of people in all the Christian churches who have lost their first love; persons who gave their hearts with joy to Christ and walked faithfully and valorously for a while, but at last dropped away. Jesus said there were several causes for this. Partly it is due to the wiles of Satan who is ever alert to snatch away the good impulses which arise in our hearts before they have time to take root and bring forth any fruit. Partly it is due to the growing monotony of life. But most of all it is due the Master thought to the deceitfulness of riches, the glitter and glamour of the things of this world.

Not long ago there was found just outside the city wall of Pompeii the body of a petrified woman with both hands full of jewels. She was fleeing from the eruption and was buried in ashes and lava. Her jewels were bracelets, necklaces, rings, amulets studded with gems, and a pair of earrings. The earrings contain twenty-one perfect pearls set in gold in imitation of a bunch of grapes. Every Christian minister has seen something analogous to this in the realm of spiritual things. He has seen young men and young women who have started well in the things of Christ, surrounded and dazed and petrified toward the higher things of life by the things which belong to this present world. It is possible that this may be true of some who read this. You look back over the past experiences of your Christian life and you realize with a certain sorrow of heart that you have lost what in the

His Long View of Life

beginning promised to be a wondrous guiding light, a source of abiding joy all your days.

The time is come for you to gather up the fragments once more that nothing be entirely lost. You have not been playing fair. You have not dealt justly with the Highest. You have been neglecting the means of God's grace, which have been appointed as the normal channels through which life is imparted to us; by which we are helped to go on keeping quite strong, and increasing in wisdom and stature all the time. Perhaps the word that needs to be said to you to-day is this: "Come back to the old things. Take again the Bible which is the Word of God, and seek in it for the revelation of God's will and love. Begin again the custom of private prayers. Start to build up again the habit of participating in the praise and worship of God in His House. Come again with a prepared and humble and penitent and contrite heart, and receive the Master in the Blessed Sacrament of His Body and Blood." It is because we neglect, or are careless concerning these things that we fall away from Christ, and miss that fine enthusiasm and continuance of strength which are the heritage of those who will learn from the Master how to watch the details of life, and to treasure up the small and seemingly insignificant, but really great elements of the provision which God has made for our support and strength.

The second foe to the grace of continuance is the impact of misfortune and sorrow. There are in general three kinds of troubles which beset us. There is adversity, or misfortune in regard to material things. I heard of a lady who at the age of 105 years had been admitted to the County Poorhouse at Grand Rapids, Michigan. In her early life she was wealthy and the hostess of such famous men as General Lafayette, the later Napoleons, King Edward VII when Prince of Wales, Kossuth, Daniel Webster, Henry Clay and others. It would seem that there might have been some other institution than the County Poorhouse for such an unusual person. But what a hardship it is to lose in middle life, and in old age particularly, the material basis upon which our life is built. How much sadness is in the phrase, "He is one who has seen better days."

There is in the second place that kind of sorrow which is described by the word bereavement, the loss out of this world and out of our lives of those who have been near and dear to us. This is a wound which is hard to heal; and oftentimes we find ourselves saying in the words of the poet, "Oh, for the touch of a vanished hand, and the sound of a voice that is still!"

In the third place there are sorrows which are perhaps more grievous and harder to bear than either of these—the sorrow of an affection that is unrequited; the service and devotion which is rejected and lightly esteemed.

Now the curious and wondrous thing about misfortune and sorrow is its varying potentialities. It is possible for trouble to enrich and ennoble. It may make the heart more tender and the mind more sympathetic. It may give us patience. It may implant in our characters elements of true godliness. Or on the other hand, it may devastate and destroy; it may lay waste the heart. It may leave the nature empty. It may make the mind lonely and bitter. It may be a voice saying to the soul, "Curse God and die."

Sometimes as the result of hardship and pain men lose their bearings. They doubt the existence of God and scoff at all goodness. But they are not in the way of happiness and peace. There is laughter perhaps, but bitterness within. The eyes that look out upon the world are defiant, but the heart is lonely, the soul is afraid. It is dark without and there is no guiding star. Here is a word straight from the heart of the Master of Life for those who are in such a sorrowful state. He cries, "Gather up the broken pieces that remain over that nothing be lost." There is still enough in your life for you to build something splendid upon. There are still those who love you. There is still some great service that you may render. There is still some desirable and attainable thing which you may strive for and which with God's help may make all the future of your life better than it ever was.

Do you remember the child's story of the artist's apprentice, the little boy who gathered up day by day, as he cleaned out the master's workshop, the small and broken waste bits of glass and stone and worked them so together that he produced a work which amazed and delighted the master artist himself? It is not, after all, in the bits of life that are given one, but in the artist spirit within, that the secret of blessing and peace is found.

It is possible for you wherever you are and whatever has been your past, however broken and wrecked and limited is your present life, to start now and gather together all the broken pieces, to find in them strength and sustenance which shall carry you on through many days, which shall be heavenly manna upon which your soul may feed and grow strong until its earth pilgrimage is over and you come to the heavenly city.

James Russell Lowell tells how once he stood at the summit of one of the Alps with a German friend. Looking toward Italy and thinking of Rome, he lifted his hat and said, "Glories of the past, I salute you." But his German friend turned away toward the north and looking toward his own fatherland, he lifted his hat and said, "Glories of the future, I salute you."

This is one of the messages from

Christ to us all. "The best is yet to be," and the way to it is in the gathering up and the treasuring and the wise using of what we have around us. We have wasted much. We have been oftentimes careless and indifferent. We have lost many opportunities. But there is still much remaining for us; still the sun is shining in the heavens for us; still the love of God abides. For us still the covenant of God's grace and mercy in the cross of Christ is effective. For us still is promised the divine assistance and blessing if we will set our faces, and follow after the Master; if we will hear and obey His voice as He cries, "Gather up the broken pieces that remain over, that nothing be lost."

V
HIS REWARD

V

HIS REWARD

WE have been studying the various attributes of Jesus' character which are illustrated in the story of the feeding of the multitude. We have seen Jesus' sense of responsibility; His resourcefulness and consciousness of a plan. We have seen His opportunism, His willingness to make the best possible use of what He had. We have seen also His sagacity and His long view of life. And now it is fair to ask at the close what Jesus Himself got out of it. We have seen what He did for others. It is natural to turn to the great worker Himself and try to discern if we can what the result of it was for Him.

The Master of the Feast

We read at the end of the narrative as it is given by St. John: "When therefore the people saw the sign which He did, they said, This is of a truth the prophet that cometh into the world. Jesus therefore perceiving that they were about to come and take Him by force, to make Him King, withdrew again into the mountain Himself alone." It is manifest at once that the reward which the populace were willing and anxious to bestow upon Jesus was one that He did not care anything about. He did not desire what they were willing to give Him. He did not wish any material reward. He had no interest in being a king.

This was not due to unselfishness, but to the fact that the kind of service He rendered was above any temporal and material reward. As a matter of fact, the glory of a great deal of service which is done in this world is that it cannot be repaid by any material thing. There is a good bit of work done which is above financial compensation, which can never be paid for in the current coin of the realm. Sometimes employers think they have done all that is required of them when they have paid their employees their wages at the end of the week. According to the standards of business, this may be true; but whoever looks faithfully upon the world of industry and commerce must perceive that there is being rendered all the time by all sorts of employees services which can never be compensated with money. There are occasions in the history of many businesses when a bookkeeper or a confidential clerk has in his hands for the time being the future destiny of the firm. There are occasions when a man stands by his friend in business and helps him through a time of storm and stress. There are many services like this which are never known. Sometimes they turn up so frequently that they become commonplace and men accept them without further thought. But we ought to recognize them and to acknowledge our gratitude for them.

Now and then when I am visiting the home of some man or other in my parish who is ill, I meet there the foreman under whom he works, or perhaps the superintendent of the shop. Sometimes the head of the firm himself will come; and I am always glad when this is so, because it is the recognition of that quality in a man which differentiates him from a mere employee.

The laboring world of our day is exceedingly ambitious for larger returns for its work. There are all sorts of plans for getting more wages. But a large part of the insistent pressure that is felt in the whole laboring world to-day arises from the desire of employees to be recognized as men and brethren. To be treated not as employees merely, but as those who render service which is above material recompense.

There is a vast amount of work going on in the world all the time which is in a very true and fine sense done with the consciousness that it is to God and not to men. It is an insult to endeavor to appraise this kind of service and to recompense it with money. When a man has risked his life to save another; when a man has strained his powers to the breaking point in the service of his employers; when a man has during a long period of time carried the secrets of the concern he works for, and has planned and endeavored to find for his concern a way out of its temporary difficulties and embarrassments, it is a shame not to recognize all that he has done in some material fashion, but it is a greater shame to think that it can be compensated with dollars and cents.

And so Jesus, after His great work of mercy and grace, felt Himself above the reward which the multitude wished to bestow upon Him. As a matter of fact the greatest services are rendered without any thought of compensation or reward. When Garibaldi the Italian patriot had gathered together his company of nondescripts and was training them into an army to go forth to fight for national freedom and unity, he stood before his men and told them what he wanted them to do; and then one of the recruits stepped forth and asked him in the name of all what he proposed to give them in return. He looked them in the face and said, "I do not know what else you will get, but I am sure that you will get hunger and cold and nakedness and wounds and some of you will get death." He looked them in the face and said those words, and in a moment they lifted up their hands and cried out together, "We are the men. We are the men."

The greatest deeds that are ever done in the way of service to others are done at the bidding of a noble inward impulse. We hear a voice speaking to us and bidding us attempt this great thing. We do not stop to consider either whether we can do the thing, or what the reward of it shall be, but we say "yes" to the voice and speed onward to the undertaking. In the great Civil War which rent our country in twain, the young men who went forth to join the armies of the North and the South went at the bidding of such a voice. It was not for the pay they were to receive as soldiers. It was not for the prospect of a good time, nor for the satisfaction of that desire for adventure which is always strong in young men's hearts. It was something underneath all this. It was love of native land and devotion to right and truth.

We ought always to remember this when we think about Christian service. The churches are filled with people who are doing inconspicuous and noble work day by day and year by year; and there are numberless institutions for the service of humanity to which men and women are giving time and thought and money ; and in the main they are doing it not with the idea of gaining notoriety or distinction of any sort, but because they have received in their hearts an impulse from that One who, though He was rich, yet for our sakes became poor, that we through His poverty might be made rich. What a multitude of workers would say, if you asked them why they were doing what they are doing, would be, "The love of Christ constraineth us; because we thus judge that one died for all—that they that live should no longer live unto themselves, but unto Him who for their sakes died and rose again."

And yet it is not an unworthy thing to raise the question as to the reward of Christian living. We Christian folk believe that there are rewards for doing good. Our Ethical Culture friends sometimes suggest that the morality of the Christian churches is not as high and pure as it should be because it countenances the thought of a reward. The best actions, they assert, are those which are done for their own sakes and with no ulterior and extraneous motives. But it is perhaps true that the Ethical Culture people are guilty of striving to wind themselves too high for sinful man beneath the sky. And it is possible that our Lord, who knew what was in man, was the wiser teacher and the better instructed Master of Living, when He spoke as He often did about the sure rewards that would come to those who endeavored to walk faithfully, and according to the light of the Spirit of God in their hearts. "Your Father which seeth in secret, Himself shall reward thee openly," He said. In the wondrous word picture of the last judgment, there is no fairer stroke than that in which the striving and serving man hears with a glad heart the welcome word of the Master saying, "Well done good and faithful servant. Enter thou into the joy of thy Lord." No. There is room in the highest and the best view of life for rewards. It is important only that we should understand what these rewards are. To understand them is to desire to be worthy to receive them.

There were two things which came to Jesus as a reward for His service that day on the hillside by the Sea of Galilee. He had the joy that comes from giving joy. He must have been conscious that this multitude of people did not understand Him very well. To many of them He was a mere wonder-worker. They could not enter into the fulness of His thoughts. They had no conception of the real purpose that He had in view for them. But they had all seen the love which was in Him, they all had been thrilled by it for a moment, and they all had been helped and blessed. He had made them happy for a while. That is a great service and a great joy.

There are people who conceive that the purpose of Christian service is to make people good. I suppose that is the ultimate aim of service. But we ought all of us to remember that no one can make anybody else good. All we can do is to put them in the way of being good. We can make them happy. Only God by His Spirit's power can make them good. And there is no joy that comes to human hearts to be compared with the joy of giving happiness.

The world is full of seekers after

joy. There are men going up and down the streets in the business sections of the great city, in and out of banks and offices and all manner of places, who are finding keen zest in the pursuit of the almighty dollar. There are women whose days are filled with all manner of social engagements. They go from one entertainment to another; from one form of diversion to another. There are people who are all for sport, and others who are all for knowledge, and some who are striving for power; but against them all and above them all I place the joy of giving joy.

There is a striking and noble passage in the Japanese Letters of Lafcadio Hearn, which have been recently published. He is speaking of the singing of Adelina Patti. It was in the St. Charles Theatre in New Orleans, and Hearn speaks of the impression that was made upon him at the moment. The great dim pressure of stifling heat; the rustle of silk; the weight of toilet perfume, "and then through all that dead hot air, the clear cool tense thread gush of melody unlike any other sound as the great Cantatrice, with no artifice and never a tremolo, sang the words of 'Auld Lang Syne.'" And then he goes on to say: "There is no song which moves me so much,—not only because of the 'intolerable pathos' (as Matthew Arnold calls it) of the words, nor only because of the souvenir of the divine voice. But there is a dream fastened to that song; the dream of an Indian city stifling in reek of pestilence and smoke of battle; trenches piled with sweltering corpses; grim preparation against worse than death; the sense of vast remoteness from all dear things; and the sudden lighting up of all those memories which grow vivid only at the last hour. And then, like one of those memories itself, startling beyond all startlingness, the Highland piping beyond the walls,—

"'We twa hae paidl't i' the burn
From morning sun till dine;
But seas between us braid have roared
Sin Auld Lang Syne.'

I believe it was first the clan call of the MacGregors; then Auld Lang Syne. What was Beethoven to that?" So it is with joy. What are all other joys compared with the joy which rises in the heart of any one who, though in humble and obscure surroundings and without great power and ability, yet with earnestness and sincerity has set himself to do an unselfish service to one who is near him? You will never know what life is until you begin to turn your abilities in the direction of such service as gives joy to others.

It is interesting and important for us to remember that the joy that comes into the human heart by service to others is not dependent upon the acknowledgment of the service by those for whom it was done. It was not necessary for Jesus, in the hour of His triumph, that the multitude should flock around Him and acclaim Him as their benefactor; should kiss His hand or kneel at His feet. He carried the joy of service in His heart. He carried it with Him when He fled from the multitude to find quiet in the mountainside.

It is good for us to know that this is so. For it is a common experience that our endeavors to give joy often fail of acknowledgment. We have to sow the seed, but the fruit is not seen until after many days. What really keeps the Christian going on is not that his service will be recognized and applauded, but the joy that he comes to have in the doing of it; a joy which exists in his heart independently of the results of his efforts.

In that sweet book of Norman Duncan's entitled "Dr. Luke of the Labrador," there is a little reminiscence of childhood, which all of us will understand. Mothers and fathers alike will recall similar experiences in their own lives. This man tells us how, when he was a boy, his mother took him on her lap and said:

"'Look in your mother's eyes, and say after me this, "My mother——"'

"'My mother,' I repeated, very soberly.

"'Looked upon my heart——'

"'Looked upon my heart,' said I.

"'And found it brave——'

"'An' found it brave——'

"'And sweet——'

"'An' sweet——'

"'Willing for the day's work——'

"'Willing for the day's work——'

"'And harboring no shameful hope——'

"'An' harboring no shameful hope.'

"Again and again she had me say it, until I knew it every word by heart.

"'Ah,' said she at last, 'but you'll forget.'

"'No, no!' I cried, 'I'll not forget. "My mother looked upon my heart," I rattled, "an' found it brave an' sweet, willing for the day's work an' harboring no shameful hope." I've not forgot! I've not forgot.'

"'He'll forget,' she whispered, but not to me, 'like all children.'

"But I have never forgotten—that, when I was a child, my mother looked upon my heart and found it brave and sweet, willing for the day's work and harboring no shameful hope."

So it is. When we come to a certain stage in our Christian life and experience, the reward of our endeavoring which we cherish is in the endeavoring itself. We go on doing good or striving to give happiness, because in that we find our greatest happiness. It is not exactly that virtue is its own reward. It is that the joy of giving joy is the great abiding comfort and outstanding happiness of our souls. As George Herbert puts it quaintly:

"Be useful where thou livest, that so men may
Both want and wish thy pleasing presence still.
Kindness, great parts, and good plans are the way
To compass this. Find out men's wants and will,
And meet them there; all worldly joys grow less,
To the one joy of doing kindliness."

There was another reward which Jesus found in the doing of His great service to the multitude. In John's account, it is said that "Jesus withdrew into the mountain Himself alone," but Matthew tells us that after Jesus had sent the multitude away, He went up into the mountain to pray. He turned away from men to God, and there in communion and fellowship with Him, He found His greatest reward.

There are two great needs of the

heart of men. First, we need happiness. We come into the world heart-hungry for joy; and the tragedy of life is that we seek it in so many false ways. We follow so many ignes fatui. There are so many false lights that gleam before us and oftentimes lead us far astray.

In addition to happiness and joy, the soul needs to find its master. We think freedom is the highest estate of man. In reality we are made for subjection. The only real question for a man is whose servant he shall be. Long ago a great saint said, "Thou O God hast made us for Thyself and our souls are restless and unhappy until we find rest in Thee." The service of God is perfect freedom. When the heart yields its submission and pledges its loyalty to the Highest, then has it achieved its crowning glory. So it was with our Lord.

The Master of the Feast

He left the multitude, clamorous with His praise. He cared alone for the praise of the Father. In the quiet and stillness of the evening, and amidst the loneliness of the fields, under the stars, He heard a voice saying, "Well done," and He was glad.

"That evening when the Carpenter swept out the fragrant shavings from the workshop floor,
  And placed the tools in order, and shut to and barred for the last time the humble door,
  And going on His way to save the world, turned from the laborer's lot forever more,
I wonder, was He glad?

"That morning when the Carpenter walked forth from Joseph's cottage in the glimmering light,
  And bade His holy mother long farewell, and through the skies of dawn all pearly bright

His Reward

Saw glooming the dark shadow of the cross ; yet seeing, set His feet toward Calvary's height,
I wonder, was He sad ?

" Ah ! when the Carpenter went on His way He thought not for Himself of good or ill,
His path was one through weary, thronging men, craving His help even to the cross-crowned hill,
Toiling, healing, loving, suffering, all His joy and life to do His Father's will,
And earth and heaven are glad."